ABDO Publishing Company

# FISH & GAME

# WHITE-TAILED DEER

Sheila Griffin Llanas

## visit us at
## www.abdopublishing.com

Published by ABDO Publishing Company, PO Box 398166, Minneapolis, MN 55439.
Copyright © 2014 by Abdo Consulting Group, Inc. International copyrights reserved in all
countries. No part of this book may be reproduced in any form without written permission from the
publisher. The Checkerboard Library™ is a trademark and logo of ABDO Publishing Company.

Printed in the United States of America, North Mankato, Minnesota.
112013
012014

 PRINTED ON RECYCLED PAPER

Cover Photo: Getty Images
Interior Photos: Alamy pp. 7, 8–9, 18, 26; AP Images p. 27; Getty Images pp. 4–5, 11, 20, 21;
    iStockphoto pp. 1, 17, 24; Science Source pp. 13, 28–29; Thinkstock pp. 19, 23;
    WILLIAM ALBERT ALLARD/National Geographic Creative p. 29

Editors: Rochelle Baltzer, Megan M. Gunderson, Bridget O'Brien
Art Direction: Neil Klinepier

### Library of Congress Cataloging-in-Publication Data

Llanas, Sheila Griffin, 1958- author.
  White-tailed deer / Sheila Griffin Llanas.
      pages cm. -- (Fish & game)
  Includes index.
  Audience: Ages 8 to 12.
  ISBN 978-1-62403-110-6
1. Hunting--Juvenile literature. 2. White-tailed deer--Juvenile literature. I. Title.
  QL737.U55L585 2014
  799.2'7652--dc23
                          2013027631

# Contents

# Deer!

Hunting is an important tradition around the world. In the United States, the favorite prize is deer. Every year, more than 10 million hunters seek deer. Just one-quarter of that number hunt for wild turkey, the second most popular animal.

White-tailed deer are one type of deer found in the United States. These animals are a top big-game species for good reasons. They are exciting to hunt. Their meat, which is called venison, is a nutritious food. And, the country has a lot of deer. More than 15 million white-tailed deer live in the United States.

*White-tailed deer are the largest wild animals that people commonly see in the United States. They are found in every state except Alaska.*

## WILD FACTS!

Not all deer hunters look for white-tailed deer. In some states, they seek mule deer, black-tailed deer, or axis deer.

White-tailed deer hunting is active in nearly every state. On average, half of all deer hunters bag a deer during the season. Deer hunting is especially popular in Pennsylvania, Texas, Wisconsin, and Michigan. Men, women, and young hunters seek deer north, south, east, and west!

# Nature in Balance

Animals need predators to keep nature in balance. Large as they are, deer are prey animals. They are hunted for food by bears, cougars, wolves, and humans.

Beginning centuries ago, Native American tribes hunted deer. To be successful, they studied deer behaviors. They learned that the animals are drawn to **decoys**. So, they dressed in deerskins and antlers to lure deer close. By hunting deer, Native Americans helped keep herds healthy.

After European explorers arrived, the deer population shrank. Fur traders sold deer hides, and pioneers wore **buckskin**. Buckskin gloves, shoes, and hats were sold. Antlers became knife handles, buttons, forks, and other

## WILD FACTS!

Deer are related to moose, elk, and caribou.

tools. As railroads crossed the nation, venison was sold to New York, Chicago, and other big cities. By the 1800s, white-tailed deer had completely disappeared from some areas.

The fur trade harmed white-tails, but the logging industry helped save them. Loggers cleared land. The newly exposed land got more sunlight, and tender green plants blossomed. Prairies and fields grew into ideal deer **habitats**. Still, too many were being hunted.

*Today, responsible hunting respects, values, and protects the nation's natural resources.*

Beginning in the late 1800s, the United States began new efforts to conserve wildlife. States hired **game wardens** and set more hunting regulations. Over time, deer populations rose again.

Today, every state guards the health of its deer and its land. So, the white-tailed deer remains a valued natural resource. Game wardens and other officials work to make sure the deer population is not too low or too high. They strive for just the right balance.

Deer need plenty of food and the right **habitat** to live in. If herds grow too large, deer compete for food. And they overgraze, which kills plants and trees. They might eat tree saplings and leave bare ground instead of new woods. In extreme conditions, deer may die of starvation.

Ultimately, too many deer can destroy a **habitat**. So, states control deer populations using information such as hunting records and population estimates. This helps determine how many deer can safely live in one area.

Deer population data also helps states decide how many deer should be hunted and other season regulations. States may set limits based on gender. For example, hunters may be asked to harvest more females than males to reduce deer populations.

Hunters must follow state rules. In return, they enjoy a healthy outdoor sport and get a supply of fresh, lean meat. Many hunters develop a deep respect for nature. They constantly learn as much as possible about white-tailed deer. And, they happily share their knowledge with others.

*Without predators, deer herds can grow out of control. So today, hunters help manage deer populations.*

# Nose to Tail

White-tailed deer are smaller in the South and larger in the North. There are at least 15 subspecies of white-tailed deer in the United States and Canada.

The largest subspecies lives from Minnesota to the East Coast and up into Canada. The smallest lives in the Florida Keys. Some Key deer stand just two feet (0.6 m) tall at the shoulders. They are listed as **endangered**, with a population of just 600 to 800.

Male white-tailed deer are called bucks. Females are called does. One clear feature sets them apart. Bucks grow antlers.

Antlers are **deciduous**. They **shed** and regrow each year. In spring, the tender new antlers are covered with a tissue called velvet. Velvet is a thin layer of skin with short, fine hairs.

## WILD FACTS!

Hunters count a deer's tines, or points. A deer with four on each antler is an 8-point buck.

Antlers grow fast, at about 0.25 inches (0.6 cm) per day. They fork and form tines. They are fully developed in four months.

Bucks can weigh 150 to more than 300 pounds (70 to more than 135 kg). Does weigh in at 90 to 200 pounds (40 to 90 kg). These big animals stand three to four feet (0.9 to 1.2 m) tall at the shoulders. They stretch six to seven feet (1.8 to 2.1 m) long.

*Geographic location, body size, color, antler growth, and other differences set apart the white-tailed deer subspecies such as the Key deer (right).*

## WHITE-TAILED DEER TAXONOMY:

Kingdom: Animalia
Phylum: Chordata
Class: Mammalia
Order: Artiodactyla
Family: Cervidae
Genus: *Odocoileus*
Species: *O. virginianus*

The white-tailed deer's scientific name is *Odocoileus virginianus*. *Odocoileus* refers to its hollow teeth. The source of its common name, white-tailed deer, is obvious! Sensing danger, a deer takes off running. Up goes the tail, showing a blaze of white. This warns others of danger and helps young deer follow their mothers.

The rest of the deer's coat is reddish-brown. There are white patches on the throat, face, tail, and stomach. In winter, the coat turns gray-brown and grows thicker. Deer hairs are hollow. This **insulates** deer from cold weather. This also keeps them **buoyant** in water. Deer are good swimmers.

On land, deer are speedy! They run as fast as 30 miles per hour (48 km/h). They spring to heights of 10 feet (3 m). Most fences are no match for deer! Deer can also jump a distance of up to 30 feet (9 m). These skills help them outrun many predators.

**WILD FACTS!**

Hunters and game wardens can tell a deer's age by how many teeth it has and how worn they are.

Due to hunting and other threats, many white-tailed deer live a year or two at most. Yet they can live as long as 15 years in the wild. In captivity, they can live 25 years.

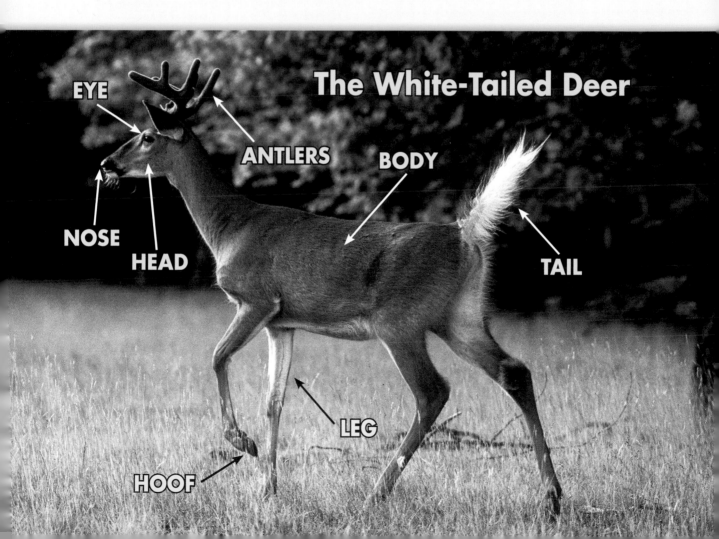

# The White-Tailed Deer

EYE

ANTLERS

BODY

NOSE

HEAD

TAIL

LEG

HOOF

# On the Edge

White-tailed deer thrive in nearly every US state. They are also found in southern Canada, Mexico, Central America, and parts of South America. They can live in many different **habitats**, including near people.

To survive, deer simply need two different types of land. They need **dense** woods for shelter. For feeding, they also need more open areas. To meet both needs, deer thrive in "edge" habitats, where two types of land meet. In fact, white-tailed deer are called "edge species."

A hickory forest near a swamp is an edge area. So is a hill near a prairie, or a park near cornfields. Edge areas are rich with a variety of plants for deer to eat.

Deer may eat in open or edge areas. After they fill their stomachs, deer hurry back to their hidden beds. For shelter, white-tails seek the dense cover of tall grasses and wooded areas. In these places, they are safer from

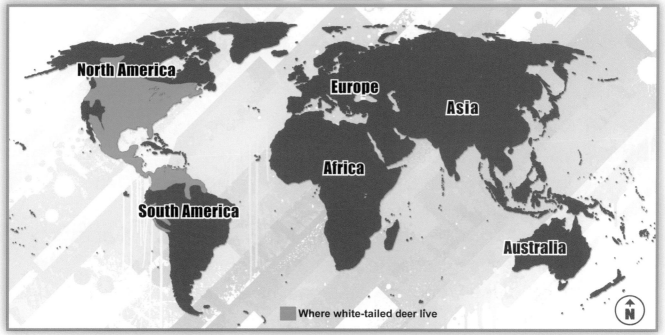

North America

Europe

Asia

Africa

South America

Australia

Where white-tailed deer live

N

predators and bad weather. When they get up, they leave oval shapes in the crushed grass, snow, or leaves.

A deer's **habitat** also needs to provide fresh water. Deer drink water from ponds, streams, and lakes. They sip dew. They also get liquid from the food they eat. In a landscape with shelter, food, and water, a white-tailed deer population can thrive.

# Herbivores

White-tailed deer are herbivores. They graze on grasses, leaves, tree saplings, and shrubs. Every day, deer eat five to nine pounds (2 to 4 kg) of whatever food is available.

The white-tailed deer's diet changes with the season. In spring, this includes tender green plants. Summer provides new farm crops. Acorns are a fall treat. In winter when food is scarce, deer gnaw on buds and twigs of woody plants.

Like cows, white-tailed deer are **ruminants** with four stomach chambers. Deer can eat quickly, storing food in the first chamber. This means less time in the open. After they hurry back to their bedding areas, they **regurgitate**, re-chew, and finally re-swallow the food.

**WILD FACTS!**

Deer can live a month without food, but they will die in three days without water.

Deer enjoy cedar, pine, maple, birch, sassafras, aspen, poplar, and fruit trees. They nibble on clover, oats, corn, beechnuts, alfalfa, prickly pear cactus, yucca, lichens, and fungi. Garden flowers and vegetables are not off limits!

Deer eat four or five meals a day. Their heaviest feeding time is from 4:30 to 7:30 PM. That is when deer are most visible.

This is a good time for hunters to stalk deer. Focused on food, deer sometimes miss warning signs. When a deer wags its tail, a hunter should stay still. That's when a deer usually lifts its head and checks for danger. If it senses something, it will lift that white tail and bolt!

# Keen Senses

*Deer move their ears to pick up noises from a specific direction, even while asleep!*

Prey animals constantly guard their safety against threats, including hunters. Having eyes placed on the sides of their heads gives them a wide field of vision. Their seven-inch (18-cm) ears act like funnels, channeling sounds to their eardrums.

A deer's sight and hearing are sharp, but its strongest sense is smell. Scientists think it is much stronger than a human's. A gust of wind sends reports of danger right into those super-keen nostrils.

Besides keen senses, deer have scent glands. The glands are on their feet, hind legs, foreheads, and eyes. When they rub up against trees, they leave their scent

*Deer may stamp their feet to leave behind a scent. This can warn others that there is danger in the area.*

behind. The odor is a form of communication. Bucks can assert their presence, establish **dominance**, or attract a mate. Does use it to find their young. Odors help family members recognize each other.

Deer also make sounds to communicate. They grunt, bleat, and whine. Sensing danger, deer snort or stamp the ground with a foot to warn other deer. When they see immediate danger, they force air through their noses and mouths. This loud, high-pitched snorting alarm sends other deer running.

# Life Cycle

*Males grow their first set of antlers at about age one.*

In fall, hunters are ready for the hunting season to begin. Deer are focused on mating season. This is called the rut. In the north, it occurs around mid-November. In the south, it occurs later.

By this time, a buck's antlers are fully grown and they have hardened. The buck rubs its head against trees and branches. It rubs so hard the velvet comes off. Tree bark does, too!

Deer go a little crazy during the rut. Bucks do not eat. Instead, they battle each other with a clash of antlers and hooves. They also chase after does. Several bucks might chase after one doe.

A single buck can mate with several does in one season. The number of does compared to bucks affects the rut and the health of deer. For example, if there are too many does, bucks may suffer stress. In this case, wildlife managers may ask hunters to harvest does.

When mating season ends, deer face a cold winter with less sunlight and food. Bucks have little energy. In a weakened state, they **shed** their antlers.

*Bucks challenge each other for territory. This decides which deer gets to mate with does in the area.*

Does that mate successfully and survive hunting season are **pregnant** for about six and a half months. Then, they give birth to one to four babies, or fawns. Twins are common.

At this time of year, there is mild weather. New spring plants are rich and nutritious. A warm climate and good food will increase a fawn's chance of survival.

At birth, fawns weigh three to six pounds (1.5 to 2.5 kg). The more they weigh, the better their chance of survival. Reddish-brown fur covered in white spots **camouflages** the fawns.

The mother nurses her fawns. But she must leave them to feed herself. To protect them from predators, she hides them. The fawns lie still and unseen in the woods, waiting for the doe to return.

Fawns are **weaned** at about six weeks. Females may stay with their mothers for two years. Males usually separate from their mothers after a year. They usually live in small groups of three to four. In winter, larger herds may form. But when mating season begins again, males live alone.

WILD FACTS!

Fawns can walk at birth!

Bucks do not typically help raise fawns.

# Safety First

*Many hunters believe it is not good sportsmanship to shoot a deer that is swimming.*

Every fall, hunters across the country enjoy the tradition of deer hunting. Hunting season overlaps with deer mating season. So in fall, deer are the most active.

Responsible hunters make sure they know all the hunting regulations before heading out into the field. Each state is different. Often, deer hunting opens 30 minutes before sunrise and ends 30 minutes after sunset.

Some states do not allow hunting on Sundays. In many places, it is illegal to use a spotlight to harvest deer. It may also be illegal to hunt from the road.

Like any sport, hunting has risks. Think safety first! Many states require gun safety courses for hunters. And in most states, hunters wear blaze-orange clothing. Hunters must be able to see other hunters! In addition, hunters should carry a map, a compass, and proper survival gear for the outdoors.

Hunters must take great care when using weapons. All firearms should be kept in good working condition. Again, states have different rules for which types of guns are allowed.

The sound of a gun firing will spook deer. This means hunters often have just one chance to get a good shot. A bow and arrow is quieter, but it has a shorter range. The hunter must get close to the target before shooting.

# On the Hunt

Hunters must find a good place to hunt deer. Trails and tracks are clues that deer are close. Deer make trails as they go from their beds to food sources. The bigger the tracks, the larger the deer! Bitten shrubs, trees, and grasses are another sign. Hunters also look for bare spots on tree trunks and gouges in the ground. Piles of scat, or deer poop, are another clear sign.

Hunters must also choose a method for hunting. Some stalk deer, quietly walking in search of the animals. They must stay downwind! Many hunters "glass" for deer, using

*In summer, deer poop about 36 times a day. That's every 45 minutes! In winter, they eat less and poop just 12 to 13 times a day.*

binoculars to spot prey. Hunters attract deer with sounds, too. They grunt and call. They also pound antlers together to make the sound of bucks fighting.

Yet success often comes by staying still in tree stands. Hunting requires patience. It can be a long wait for deer to come within range.

When a hunter spots a deer, he takes aim and shoots. The best result is a clean, fatal shot. If a wounded deer runs, the hunter must track it. Hunters then approach the deer with caution and make sure it has died. Then, they unload their weapons, and begin to get the deer ready to take home.

*Hunters must be very careful with firearms in a tree stand.*

# Day's End

Now a new level of work begins. The deer must be tagged, **field dressed**, and transported. From this point forward, the body must be handled carefully. The venison must be kept clean and cool.

In most states, deer hunters must report every deer killed. On the tag, the hunter notes information such as the animal's sex, the date, the time of kill, the weapon used, and the location. The tag is attached to the deer's antler or leg.

Then it's time to field dress the deer. This takes a sharp knife, gloves, a strong stomach, and an adult's help. Hunters hang

*Hunters appreciate the challenge a white-tailed deer provides.*

something blaze orange to indicate their presence to other hunters. Then, they remove the animal's organs while being careful to avoid spreading bacteria.

To carry the deer back to a vehicle or camp, the deer can be dragged by hand for short distances. For longer distances, the deer can be hauled with a sled, wheelbarrow, or other device.

For the deer hunter, the season is over. Deer hunting is hard work. It requires preparation, patience, and caution. It takes skill and responsibility. Nationwide, deer hunters embrace the sport. As soon as one hunting season ends, they start thinking about the next one!

# Glossary

**buckskin** - a soft, bendable leather made from the skin of a buck.

**buoyant** (BOY-uhnt) - able to float.

**camouflage** (KA-muh-flahzh) - a disguise or way of hiding something by covering it up or changing its appearance.

**deciduous** (dih-SIH-juh-wuhs) - falling off each year.

**decoy** - someone or something used to lure another into a trap.

**dense** - closely packed together or crowded.

**dominance** - importance or power, especially of one person or animal over another.

**endangered** - in danger of becoming extinct.

**field dressing** - the task of removing an animal's internal organs after it has been taken by a hunter.

**game warden** - a person in charge of protecting wildlife.

**habitat** - a place where a living thing is naturally found.

**insulate** - to keep something from losing heat.

**pregnant** - having one or more babies growing within the body.

**regurgitate** (ree-GUHR-juh-tayt) - to throw back out again, especially partly broken-down food.

**ruminant** (ROO-muh-nuhnt) - a type of mammal that chews cud and has a three- or four-chambered stomach.

**shed** - to cast off hair, feathers, skin, or other coverings or parts by a natural process.

**wean** - to accustom an animal to eating food other than its mother's milk.

To learn more about white-tailed deer, visit ABDO Publishing Company online.  Web sites about white-tailed deer are listed on our Book Links page.  These links are routinely monitored and updated to provide the most current information available.

**www.abdopublishing.com**

# Index